Purpose, Career And Business Analytics: A Workbook For Discovering Your Purpose, Choose The Right Career & The Best Businesses You Are Designed To Do

MOSES OMOJOLA

Copyright © 2018 Moses Omojola

All rights reserved.

ISBN-10: 1987775260
ISBN-13: 978-1987775266

DEDICATION

To God Almighty.

CONTENTS

Introduction — 1

Chapter 1: What Is Purpose, Career & Business Analytics — 7

Chapter 2: How To Develop Your Own Purpose, Career & Business Analytics — 9

Chapter 3: Generating Data For Your Purpose, Career & Business Analytics I — 11

Chapter 4: Evaluating The Data For Your Purpose, Career & Business Analytics I — 15

Chapter 5: Generating Data For Your Purpose, Career & Business Analytics II — 21

Chapter 6: Evaluating The Data For Your Purpose, Career & Business Analytics II — 25

Chapter 7: Developing Your Own Personalized Life Purpose/Career/Business Profile — 31

Chapter 8: Strategizing Your Discovered Life Purpose, The Unique Career Words And The Businesses — 37

Chapter 9: Author's Final, Referrals & Recommendations — 39

ACKNOWLEDGMENTS

Appreciation to all my teachers and students all over the world.

INTRODUCTION

Studies say over 85% of workers in their jobs are on the wrong jobs, leading to abject poverty (physical or health-wise), sickness, frustration, and early death.

STOP OPERATING BELOW YOUR DESIGNED CAPACITY. DISCOVER YOUR LIFE PURPOSE, CAREER & BUSINESS NOW.

Job is undefined – set by the world system as a way of making ends meet. Work is the ultimate – leading to fulfillment, real success, real wealth, health and longevity.

THE AGONY OF JOB

❖ **Writing name with conventional and unconventional hands!**

> **OBSERVATION!** When you do something not natural to you...
> 1. You felt uncomfortable.
> 2. It took extra time and effort.
> 3. You still did a bad job on it!
> ❑ This happens when you operate in areas that are not suited for your make up.

■ Confusion, frustration, <u>poverty (lack of inner peace, health)</u>, stress, & early death.

➢ Job - a **betrayal of the heart**. Job is a sword piercing the heart daily.

➢ Circum navigation **(Straight walk into your Destiny)**
  ❑ **Israelites**, fruitless effort in wilderness (Purposeful walk: 2 weeks)

■ Sweat - pushing an immovable wall. F cross D = 0, total work done = zero

■ Job is an **endless search due to frustration**.

Everyone needs to know the direction the pendulum of his life is swinging. That's not enough. One must question himself by asking quizzically, is that the real direction my life is divinely designed to swing for real success, wealth, good health and fulfillment?

DESTINY AND GRASSHOPPER IMAGE

"in all these things we are more than conquerors through him that loved us" (Rom 8:37KJV).
- The power of vision: Vision: **Bigger than you. Gives you boldness**
- You can do it.
- Even the enemy of your father's house cannot stop you. **Because it's God's project.**
- Knowing who you are gives you self-confidence
- **Millions mourned, yet Grapes, how? Thank God for Caleb and Joshua. Numbers 13.**
- PETER was a coward until the day of Pentecost when he caught vision.

At this point, the three questions below become relevant:

Where am I presently?

Where do I suppose to be (destination)?

How do I get to where I suppose to be (my destination)?

When you ask yourself the three questions above, it means you are getting closer to taking meaningful decisions about your precious life.

YOUR MESSAGE
(Your product)

In this dilemma, you see yourself becoming more worried and focused than before. You want to take an assessment of your life journey so far; physically, emotionally and spiritually.

NOW LET'S PONDER ON THESE:
SPIRITUAL INFORMATION AND IN/FORMATION
Good "grasp" on your bible
- But still confused about life.

Hence this book will offer great help to those who want to:

- Become genuinely self employed
- Discover their born identity, destiny (life purpose), and find their way to sustainable wealth
- Step out of confusion regarding what work or business to do
- Know the real work, career and business they are uniquely created to do, get trained and start them.
- Cast their true life vision and have more than five sources of income.
- Overcome depression, stress, disability, chronic sickness, guilt, addiction & divorce.
- Overcome lack of inner peace, health & fulfillment.

In the totality of this exercise, it will enable you develop for yourself a personalized Life Purpose (Destiny)/career/Business Profile (your life manual or divine assignment guide) containing the details of the career and businesses only you was created to do, how to start them and succeed. This package will transform your life, business and health in a way you never imagined.

This profile will show you all that are recommended for you to have satisfaction, fulfillment, and true success in life.

Furthermore, this workbook will move you from wrong jobs to real work, help you identify your niche and love yourself, plan for your future and children, get the right employment and have work satisfaction (not job satisfaction), eliminate confusion & invest in the right business, eliminate stress, hypertensions & outrageous fitness bills. You will begin to build wealth, have peace, high self esteem and good health.

Summarily, this workbook carefully guides you to have full understanding of what your life purpose is, the most appropriate career for you based on your uniqueness, and map out 3-7 best businesses you are designed to do convincingly.

Chapter 1

WHAT IS PURPOSE, CAREER & BUSINESS ANALYTICS

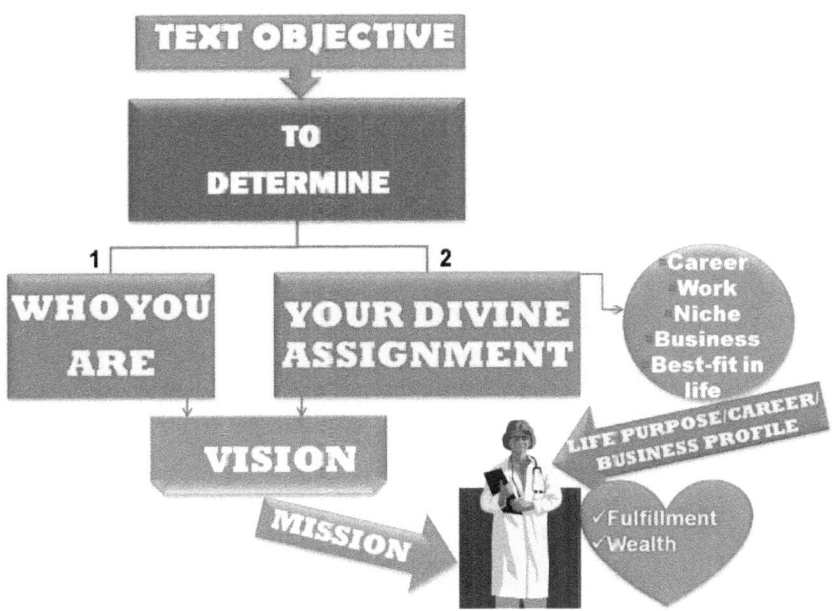

Purpose, career and business analytics refers to a systemic approach in which vital information – a life manual guide called "Professionally Analyzed Personalized Life Purpose (Destiny)/career/Business Profile – that will help someone fulfill his purpose, choose the right career and live it, discover 3-7 best businesses he is designed to do passionately and make money, are been developed through systematic psychoanalysis of data that brings out the uniqueness of such individual by comparative analysis and modern predictive modeling.

Chapter 2

HOW TO DEVELOP YOUR OWN PURPOSE, CAREER & BUSINESS ANALYTICS

To enable you develop your own business analytics as accurate as possible, you will come across many inventories, psychometric resources in this book. These are tools carefully assembled to make you arrive at mandatory decisions regarding your life, and in particular your life purpose, career and business pursuit.

This class exercise is divided into two parts. The first set of psychometric tools focuses revealing who you are, your make up or uniqueness. That is, those things that set you apart from any other person on planet earth. The second part of the psychometric tools help provide additional data that will convincing lead to determining your true personality, life purpose, career and businesses. It reveals the recommended parameters you should follow to enable her live your life in such a way that you will have satisfaction, wealth, fulfillment, significance and true success in life.

Caution

1. You are expected to provide honest short answers/fill-ins in each case.
2. Be informed that your effort in providing a honest assessment of yourself forms the core of the entire process of helping yourself discover your life purpose, right career and 3-7 businesses that best fit you.
3. Plan yourself and excuse yourself to a quiet environment that will enable you to think deeply about yourself and your past experiences, and put down the best answer each time as expected.
4. To every question or statement, think deep and put down the exact answer, making it as short as you can.
5. Comprehensive instructions will be given to you on each of the inventories.
6. You may answer directly on your computer on the same inventory pages or externally.

Chapter 3

GENERATING DATA FOR YOUR PURPOSE, CAREER & BUSINESS ANALYTICS I
(Discovering your make-up (uniqueness/who you are))

Kindly follow the instructions preceding each exercise and complete the exercises.

A. CIRCLE YOUR BEST 5 AT MOST in order of preference, indicating 1st choice, 2nd, 3rd…

<u>I love to…</u>
Design and develop•Pioneer•Organize•Serve/Help•Acquire and possess• Excel• Influence• Perform• Improve•Repair• Lead and be in charge• Operate/Maintain•Persevere•Follow the rules• Prevail.

B. WHICH 5 – 10 OUT OF THESE DO YOU THINK YOU POSSESS?

In order of preference, indicate 1st choice, 2nd, 3rd, 4th,

5th… above each of them.

Entertaining ability• Recruiting• Artistic• Graphics• Evaluating• Planning• Managing• Analyzing• Building• Coaching• Computing• Communicating• Connecting•Consulting•Cooking•Coordinating• Designing•Developing•Interview•Researching• Directing•Editing•Encouraging•Engineering• Facilitating• Forecasting• Implementing• Improving• Influencing•Leading•Learning•Mentoring• Operating•Organizing•Performing•Pioneering• Performing•Promoting•Counseling•Teaching• Resourcing•Serving•Strategizing•Translating• Traveling•Visualizing•Welcoming•Motivating• Negotiating• Writing• Feeding• Recall• Mechanical operating•Resourceful• Counting• classifying• Public Relations•Composing•Landscaping•Decorating ability.

C. WHICH 1-5 OF THESE DESCRIBES YOUR PERSON? UNDERLINE THEM.

Indicate 1st choice, 2nd, 3rd, 4th and 5th above each of them in order of preference.

I am:

Bold•Talkative•Compassionate•Decisive•

Empathetic•Hospitable•Steadfast•Eager•Accommodating•Careful•Self-assured• Enthusiastic• Loyal•Precautionary•Venturesome•Easygoing• Orderly• Organized• Persuasive• Responsive• Open Minded• Mild• Sincere• Restless• Big picture Oriented•Gentle•Quiet•Humble•Earnest•Fast paced•Freewheeling•Meek•Reserved•Intense• Visionary• Yielding•Shy• Results focused• Flexible• Meticulous.

F. GO THROUGH THE FOLLOWING LIST AND <u>UNDERLINE</u> THE ONES THAT DESCRIBE YOUR PERSON.

Professional Services

Medical, Lifeguard, Legal, Law enforcement, Accounting, Engineer, Technician, Counseling, Unemployment, Marketing, Public relations, Advertising, Television station worker, Radio station worker, Computer programming, Journalist/Writer, Human resources, Catering, Construction, Architect, Interior design/decorator, Artist, Musician, Transportation, Sports.

Office Skills, Multi Media and Theatrical

Word processing, Receptionist, Data Entry, Library, Audio Production, Lighting, Video Editing, Video Control Room, Camera Operator, Instrumentalist, Actor/Actress, Poet, Dancer, Set Construction,

Playwright, Theatre Director, Music Director.

Kindly List other skills, interest, talents, abilities, or unique opportunities that you have below:

_____

Chapter 4

EVALUATING THE DATA FOR YOUR PURPOSE, CAREER & BUSINESS ANALYTICS I

This chapter helps you analyze the <u>information you put down about yourself</u> in chapter 3 of this book **[Generating data for your purpose, career & business analytics I]**

To enable you analyze this information you put down about yourself, I have included Mr Mike Case Study as a guide example. Mr Mike is one of the numerous clients I helped discovered their destiny (life purpose), chose the right career for and discovered the 3-7 businesses that they are best designed to do, and showed how they can start them. In fact, I personally did the analysis and extrapolation for Mr Mike as shown below after he provided his own answers to the same inventories displayed above in this book.

In Mr Mike example shown below, <u>the words marked red</u> were inserted by me as a clue to arriving at the cumulative results that will lead to determining Mr

Mike's unique life purpose, right career and best business to do.

Also, <u>the words and phrases underlined</u> below by me showed areas that needed emphases, consideration and concentration of thought.

Now, kindly go through your answers and do something similar to those shown in Mr Mike Case Study 1 below.

MR MIKE CASE STUDY 1

A. Choose 5 from 15, indicating 1st, 2nd, 3rd...
I love to:
1st Pioneer [Pacesetter, starting new project, faith for success]
2nd Perform
3rd Serve/Help
4th Design & Develop
5th Acquire & Possess [Procurement]

B. Choose 5-11 from 60 Indicating 1st, 2nd, 3rd...
1st Communicating [Talk show/Music live performance]
2nd Performing
3rd Promoting [Help the afflicted]
4th Writing [Song]
5th Visualizing [Creative thinking, imaginative thinking]
6th Artistic [Medium of expression]
7th Managing [Run the show]
8th Encouraging [The needy]
9th Facilitating (making possible) [Procure for the needy]
10th Pioneering [Faith to start new thing]
11th Relations (able to build relationships) [Solicit & Advocate for the needy]

C. Choose 1-5 from 41 Indicating 1st, 2nd, 3rd...
1st Talkative
2nd Compassionate

3rd <u>Persuasive</u> [Advocate, a funny man put people to laughter, before they recover from the laughter, he tenders a request. This request is granted before the donors recover themselves].
4th Meticulous

D. Choose 5 from <u>28</u>. Indicating 1st, 2nd, 3rd…
1st <u>Music</u>
2nd <u>Prayer</u>
3rd <u>Prophecy</u>
4th <u>Teaching</u>
5th <u>Mercy/Compassion</u>

E. MR MIKE'S VERIFIED GIFT

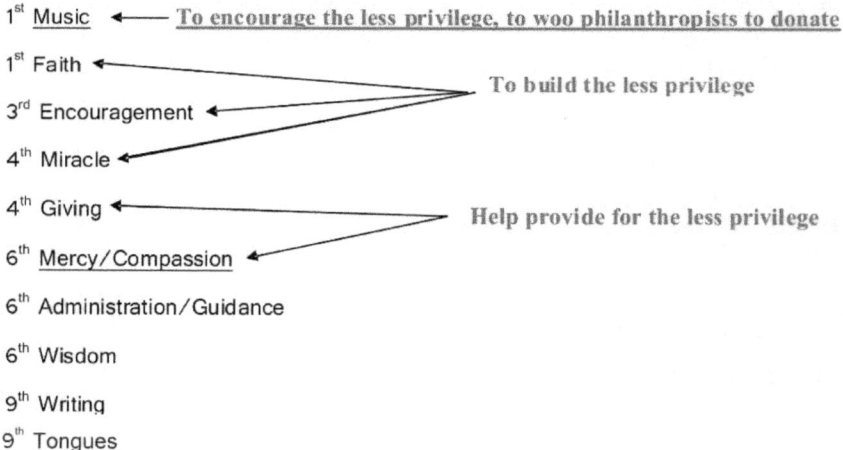

PURPOSE, CAREER AND BUSINESS ANALYTICS

F. Marketing

Public relations

Advertising

Musician

Audio production

Instrumentalist

OTHERS (Self-suggested):

Copy writing

Song writing

Singing & Performing

Advocacy for the afflicted

Music studio products
(Meeting the emotional, physical, and spiritual needs of the afflicted)

By careful analysis, look through the data you put down from inventories in chapter 4, and formulate your own (1) UNIQUENESS, M. A. M (2) M - MESSAGE, A - ASSIGNMENT and M - MEDIUM OF ASSIGNMENT similar to Mr Mike's own show below:

[MR. MIKE'S UNIQUENESS]

Summation

- Music, Guidance, Wisdom

- Pioneering. Encouragement,

- Performing, Singing, Creativity

- Communicating, Humorous, Persuasive

- Poet, Copy Writer

{MIKE's M.A.M}

- Encouragement
- Compassion – Giving
- Music, Advisory

Chapter 5

GENERATING DATA FOR YOUR PURPOSE, CAREER & BUSINESS ANALYTICS II

<u>DISCOVERING YOUR DIVINE ASSIGNMENT:</u>
(Your Unique Businesses, Divine work, Career, Best-fit in life, Destiny function, Destiny forms, Niche) {What to be sought for in life, not to sought for}

Kindly provide answer to the following statement:

1. If I knew I won't fail, this is what I would attempt to do for God with my life:
2. Jobs or skills I have experience in:
3. I have taught a class or seminar on (state topic):
4. I feel my most valuable personal asset (skill or asset) is:
5. Who I love to work with most, and the age, and type of people:
6. Church issues, ministry, society, community or possible needs that excite or concern me most:
7. My current job is:
8. Seminars or training that has been meaningful to me:

9. My ministry experience (where I have served in the past (List name of church or religious organization, position held and years of service).
10. My service to humanity/working experience (where I have served in the past). List out names of companies or institution, position held and years involved.
11. What did you study in the University, College or at Craft school?
12. What course did you regret you didn't read?
13. What career/profession are you deeply involved in now?

*THE RIDDLE OF WHAT YOU STUDIED AND DID NOT STUDY

- Establish and explain the riddles of what you studied and what you wish you had studied.

14. What breaks my heart? (What do you hate in the society or like to correct, I mean what bothers you?)
15. What need would I like to see met?
16. a) I have a dream that:
    b) I have burden for:
    c) My friends would say I care most about:
    d) If money were no objection (hindrance) I would:
    e) When _____ comes up in conversation I could talk all night. **MUSIC**
    f) The most fun (excitement) I ever had "volunteering" was:

X1. People group you would like to help most. (Please indicate 1st, 2nd, 3rd, etc.):
Adults, Children, Infants, Single parents, Students, Family, College, Next Generation, Elderly, Homeless, Hospitalized, Divorced, Unemployed, AIDS patients, Abuse victims.
Other _____

X2. Issues you are most concerned about? (9). (Please indicate 1st, 2nd, 3rd, etc.):
Environment, Education, Health care, Injustice, Mission, Poverty, Evangelism, Addictions

Others _____

X3. Function or value of highest priority to you? (13). (Please indicate 1st, 2nd, 3rd, etc.):
Worship, Prayer, Compassion, Artistic Expression, Mentoring, Learning, Relationships, Connecting people, Music, Organizing, Technology, creating systems.

g) Summarize your thoughts into a sentence that identifies how you would like to make a difference or contribution to the world:
I have a heart for: _____
[Your Mission Statement/Life Vision]

MOSES OMOJOLA

Chapter 6

EVALUATING THE DATA FOR YOUR PURPOSE, CAREER & BUSINESS ANALYTICS II

MR MIKE CASE STUDY 2

This chapter helps you analyze the <u>information you put down about yourself</u> in chapter 5 of this book [Workbook For Generating Data For Your Purpose, Career & Business Analytics II {<u>Discovering your divine assignment</u> (Your Unique Businesses, Divine work, Career, Best-fit in life, Destiny function, Destiny forms, Niche) (What to be sought for in life, not to sought for)

To enable you analyze this information you put down about yourself, I have included Mr Mike Case Study as a guide example. Mr Mike is one of the numerous clients I helped discovered their destiny (life purpose), chose the right career for and discovered the 3-7 businesses that they are best designed to do, and showed how they can start them. In fact, I personally did the analysis and extrapolation for Mr Mike as shown below after he provided his own answers to the same inventories displayed above in this book.

In Mr Mike example shown below, the words marked red were inserted by me as a clue to arriving at the cumulative results that will lead to determining Mr Mike's unique life purpose, right career and best business to do.

Also, the words and phrases underlined below by me showed areas that needed emphases, consideration and concentration of thought.

Now, kindly go through your answers and do something similar to those shown in Mr Mike Case Study below.

1. **Writing,** Creating **and** performing inspired Gospel music **for God.**
2. Advertising, **Writing, Graphic designs,** Music production and performance, Marketing, branding **and** public relations.
3. **Corporate** advertising **and** gifts **items** production
4. **My** marketing ability [Persuading donors]
5. **{The youth,** those with music related gifts}
6. a) **That Christian will** embrace gospel music **rather than secular music.**
   b) **That the** helpless and homeless, **especially the insane should be** cared for.

7. Graphic communications and Corporate Diary and Stationery production

[Paul told us communication means giving to the needy:

8. a) Towards better advertising practice
   b) Covenant faith Bible Institute
   c) National Oil and Gas Conference, London

[To learn how to procure for the less privilege]

9. a) Church = Choir Coordinator = 2005 – 2007 = 2years
   b) Sunday School = Teacher = 2007 – 2012 = 5 years

10. a) NYSC Secondary School   Teacher
    1985
    b) Ludac Sings Ltd   Studio
       Manager   1986
    c) Rock – Forte Ltd   Copy writer
       1987   [Advertising]
    d) Vantage Advertising Ltd   Copy writer/
       Client Service Executive [errand boy]

11. History / Political Science
12. Mass Communications / Music / Theatre arts
    [Live it; telling the rich about the less privilege]
13. Graphic Communications, Printing, Branding & Marketing Services [Make helping the less privilege attractive]

THE RIDDLE OF WHAT YOU STUDIED AND DID NOT STUDY

HISTORY means: Rewriting the unpleasant part of history. This means changing the life of people that many have rejected in the society.

POLITICAL SCIENCE means: **a crowd gatherer and motivator**
[Talk show, Concert, Presentation]

BRANDING means: Repackaging or rebranding the less privilege to become someone in life.

14. Injustice to fellow human beings; especially abandonment of mad people on the street.
15. That every poor person has the financial well-withal to meet his needs.
16. a) Gospel music should be widely accepted like secular music.
[Jesus sent to the lost sheep of house of Israel by Vision, but extended it to the Gentiles by Mission: Sing not only faith then, sing love and Justice]
b) **The** downtrodden**, the** rejected**, the** homeless**,** the poor **and the** mad people **on the streets.**
c) **Making money.** [To do what? To help the less privilege/mentally derailed people]
d) **Like to** set up **the biggest successful Gospel music entertainment company in Nigeria.**

[What do you want to sing about? Make people know that Deliverance (Salvation) is through compassion, justice, faithfulness and giving.

e) MUSIC
f) Coordinating **my Church** Choir **for 3 years.**
[Music]
X1. Students, Infants, Homeless**, Abused victims, Unemployed**
Others: Mad people.
[Tailor your programme to suit your particular audience]
X2. Poverty & Injustice. [Talking and Singing about]
X3. Music, Artistic expression, Compassion, **Prayer, Learning,** Relationship.
[Artistic expression, Music, Relationship and Compassion]
g) I have a heart for:
Using Creative ideas to solve the problems of poverty, helplessness and injustice in the world.
[Mission Statement]

Chapter 7

DEVELOPING YOUR OWN PERSONALIZED LIFE PURPOSE/CAREER/BUSINESS PROFILE

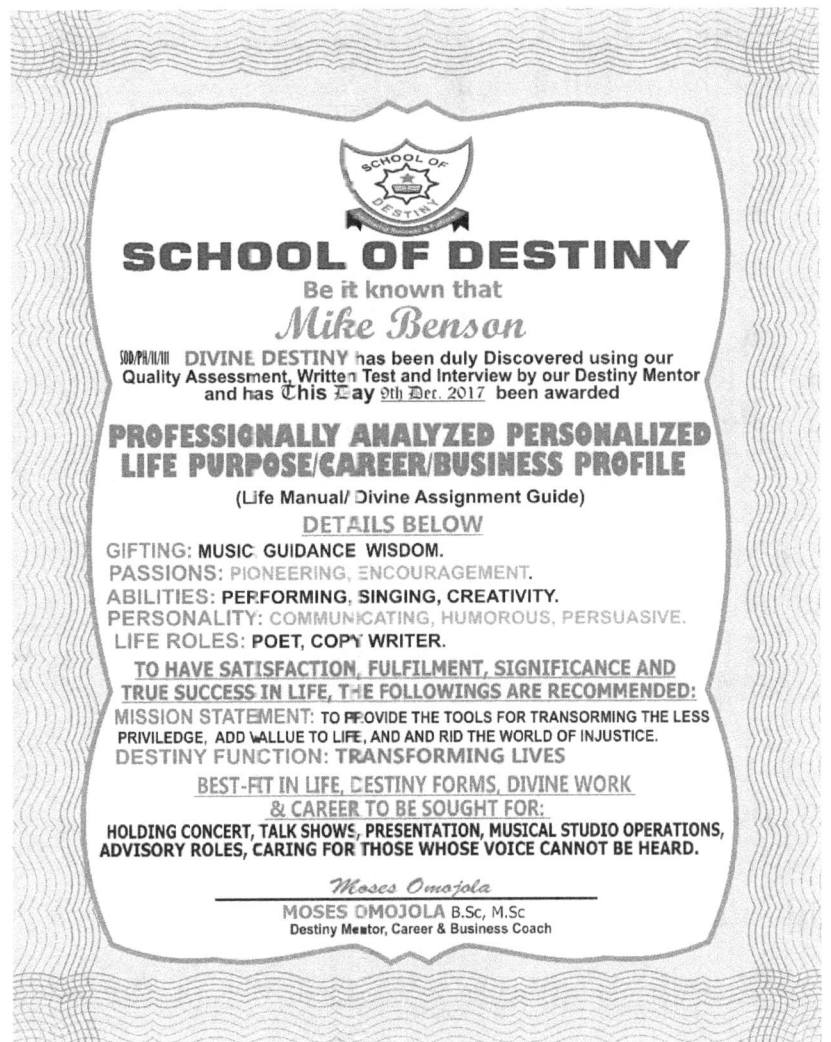

The main objective of the Purpose, Career and

Business Analytics is to equip you to develop a personalized Life Purpose (Destiny)/Career/Business profile for you to be able to journey through life more smoothly by having good understanding of yourself, loving your unique career and doing 3-7 businesses you are specially designed to, thereby attaining real success, good health and fulfillment.

To arrive at this, examine all the evaluation you've made before now. Whatever you believe in:

Step 1: Invite the Spirit of God to help you in analyzing the data and be accurate in your decisions.
Step 2: Take note of repeated characters and extract your real make –up (who you are or uniqueness).
Step 3: Extract your life mission statement from the divine assignment inventories.
Step 4: Extract all your divine tasks from the divine assignment inventory.
Step 5: Reconcile your make-up with your mission statement.

Now, develop your own Personalized Life Purpose/Career/Business Profile as Mr Mike's profile shown below:

MR MIKE PERSONALIZED LIFE PURPOSE (DESTINY)/CAREER/BUSINESS PROFILE
(Life Manual/Divine Assignment Guide)
DETAILS BELOW

TO HAVE SATISFACTION, FULFILMENT, SIGNIFICANCE AND TRUE SUCCESS IN LIFE THE FOLLOWING ARE RECOMMENDED:

MISSION STATEMENT: To provide the tools for transforming the less privilege, add value to life and rid the world of injustice.

MESSAGE: Encouragement [This will come from your verified gift]

ASSIGNMENT/NICHE: Compassion - Giving [This will come from your verified gift]

MEDIUM OF EXPRESSION: Music, Advisory [This will come from your verified gift]

UNIQUE BUSINESSES TO BE SOUGHT FOR (Divine work, Career, Best-fit in life, Destiny forms, Niche, Businesses, Investment area)
Holding concert, Talk shows, Presentation, Musical studio operations, Advisory roles, Caring for those whose voice cannot be heard (Charity & Advocacy NGO tagged "It could be me foundation") [This will come from overall analysis of all your results]

The above 6 tasks are the areas Mr Mike has been designed and divinely ordained to function best in life. These 6 tasks contain his life purpose, right career to pursue and the best businesses to do in life to become successful, also the areas to invest funds in life.

When these 3 tasks are considered: Holding concert, Talk shows, Presentation, Musical studio operations. It suggests that if Mr Mike wants to go to high college or university, he should study Mass Communication or theatre arts. Best option is mass communication so that he would be able to function well in life in his designed areas: Holding concert, Talk shows, Presentation, Musical studio operations. He can also do a short course on music and instrumentals.

HOW TO INTERPRET LIFE PURPOSE(DESTINY)/CAREER/BUSINESS PROFILE

It takes supernatural wisdom to develop a professionally analyzed life purpose(destiny)/career/business profile, and also takes great supernatural wisdom to interpret it appropriately.

I interpreted Mr Mike profile as below and also issued him an audio cd version of it comprehensively.

MR MIKE'S LIFE PURPOSE (DESTINY)/CAREER/BUSINESS PROFILE

DETAILS AS DEVELOPED BY ME AND REVEALED TO ME:

- Mr Mike is called into Compassion – Giving assignment.
- To gather people using music and advisory as medium.
- Organize concert; Music tune: Compassion, giving and love.
- Organizing talk show city to city and abroad. Encouraging people to give to the poor.
- Invite meaningful people to concert, including government officials and philanthropists.
- Run compassion related show, including talk show.
- Device methods to get money from the rich to the less privilege (procurement).
- You will also organize show for the less privilege, and in their domain.
- Persuasive talks to make people donate to the less privilege.
- Raise "It could be me foundation". Write songs, sing world unification songs.
- Link concert to attendees receiving their miracles as they attend.
- Run a music studio where you teach youth and adult music.
- Compose advertising songs for corporate companies and sell them.

- Venture into complete music recording and video shooting.
- Sourcing for the less privilege needs and holding concert and pressing the right button, approaching the right offices, you will be surprise at what God will do, etc.

Chapter 8
STRATEGIZING YOUR DISCOVERED LIFE PURPOSE, THE UNIQUE CAREER AND THE BUSINESSES

After developing your life purpose(destiny)/career/business profile, you now have a clear understating of what to do in life, moreso, where to concentrate your energy and achieve uncommon results.

You now take a look at all your revealed life task, in case of Mr Mike 6. Think and do research likely on google to dig deep into each of the businesses or career. Know what it takes to go into each of the businesses, including the needed training. What next? You decide which of them you can start first most conveniently and with least starting capital. This is how you strategize.

Chapter 9

AUTHOR'S FINAL WORDS, REFERRALS & RECOMMENDATIONS

GET YOUR

"PROFESSIONALLY ANALYZED PERSONALIZED LIFE PURPOSE(DESTINY)/CAREER/BUSINESS PROFILE"

DEVELOPED BY ME DIRECTLY! (Just $75)

Contact me on this email: *reflects2015@gmail.com*

Kindly read below to know why you need it, and to see other relevant information:

MANDATE & COMMISSION

- God commissioned me in a heavenly vision to teach Divine Assignment and purpose living life-style across the whole World.

- He gave me heavenly wisdom to unravel the mystery called Destiny (life purpose).
- Guide people in choosing right career and best fit businesses.
- Expose hidden truth about the Concept of Job and Work.
- Place people on the right work, career and business.
- Make people understand themselves much better physically, emotionally and spiritually.

Friend, I have given you my most valued resources in this book with the aim that you will be able to develop your personalized life purpose/destiny/career/business profile on your own, and begin to live your life to the fullest, doing what you love, making money while adding value to lives.

I called the profile you will develop from the guide in this book your **"Basic Personalized Life Purpose (Destiny)/Career/Business Profile"**.

I know you are intelligent, but the sent knows more the hearer. You can try on your own to develop your **basic profile**. However, for sure you won't be able to do it comprehensively as I would have done it for you. Why? This is because I am the one God commissioned to help individuals discover this all over the world. When God gave me this assignment, to run seminar all over the world on this, I asked Him to empower me to write the book I will be giving attendees. And he poured his awesome grace upon me to write my first book on this field in 2010 titled: **"How To Discover Your Destiny And Total Breakthroughs"** which I did. I encourage you to buy the book on Amazon and read.

To BUY **"How To Discover Your Destiny And Total Breakthroughs on Amazon"**, click here: https://www.amazon.com/-/e/B00CMUMQ08

That book is great! However, after writing that book, God has poured wisdom that is more than 10 times the one contained in that book into my life, yet you can't read that book and not thank God on my behalf exceedingly.

After you read this book you are reading now, and you <u>contact me through my Email</u> to help you develop your own profile for you, the one I will develop for you will be called:

<u>*"Professionally Analyzed Personalized Life Purpose(Destiny)/Career/Business Profile"*.</u>

<u>The following are the benefits you will get when I personally develop your professionally analyzed life purpose*(Destiny)*/career/business profile for you:</u>

- You will have one-on-one personal encounter with me.

- Due to online publishing policies and plagiarism control requirement, activities D and E exercises have been removed to enable this book published, so you can only get access to them by contacting me directly.
- It will enable you ask me some questions concerning any area in this workbook you don't understand.
- I will forward the complete inventories and the psychometric tools directly to your email box.
- When you forward back to me your answer sheet by email, I will go through your answers. Those questions or questionnaires you responded wrongly to, I will communicate with you verbally, by email and whatsapp, asking you some questions by way of interview and clarification to ensure that your final life purpose/career/business profile are exactly what it should be.
- It will enable you get me develop professionally analyzed life purpose/career/business profile for members of your family and friends.
- I will get you accurate analysis of your supplied data, evaluation and rightly interpret the information you supplied and reveal who you are comprehensively.

- You will have access to more opportunities and some gifts from me.
- And lots more.

You will pay just 75 Dollars ($75) for this service instead of the $250 I charge during my live seminars/workshops.

You are to pay this money to me preferably by PayPal.

Upon payment, I will forward all inventories and the psychometric tools to you by email. You can insert your answers direct through your computer, or better still, get separate sheet of paper to carefully put down your answer. You will then scan the answer sheets, and send them to me by email.

Upon receiving your answer sheets, **within 7 days**, I will analyze your provided answers, by the divine grace given to me to carry out this assignment for people like you. I will then commune with my spirit, your spirit and God's Spirit and graciously develop your **"Professionally analyzed personalized life purpose (destiny)/career/business profile"** in a way that will beat your imagination.

Send your request for **"Professionally Analyzed**

Personalized Life Purpose(Destiny)/Career/Business Profile" to me through this Email Address:

Email Address: reflects2015@gmail.com

Just $75 now for a limited time.

Act now while offer last!

Send me a mail now.

ABOUT THE AUTHOR

I am the author of the famous book: "How to discover your divine destiny and total breakthroughs" and many other great books. I spent 16 years working as Engineer in the Oil and Gas industry before I was divinely conscripted into my divine assignment. I am an author, international speaker, counselor, life purpose, career and business coach.

I run workshops helping people discover their life purpose, the unique businesses and career they are designed to do, how to start them and succeed. I also counsel indivicuals empathetically on issues relating to life purpose, employment, health, relationships, and many more, using the awesome power inherent in their destiny, and assist many to discover themselves.

www.ingramcontent.com/pod-product-compliance
Lightning Source LLC
Chambersburg PA
CBHW070420230526
45471CB00006B/2909